D1466231

HIGHLIGHTS OF NASCAR RACING™

GREAT MOMENTS IN NASCAR RACING

SALLY GANCHY

rosen publishing's
rosen central®

New York

To Jeffrey Spaulding, the world's most handsome and charming explorer

Published in 2008 by The Rosen Publishing Group, Inc.
29 East 21st Street, New York, NY 10010

"NASCAR" is a registered trademark of the National Association for Stock Car Auto Racing, Inc.

Library of Congress Cataloging-in-Publication Data

Ganchy, Sally.
Great moments in NASCAR racing / Sally Ganchy. — 1st ed.
    p. cm. — (Highlights of NASCAR racing)
Includes bibliographical references and index.
ISBN-13: 978-1-4042-1397-5 (library binding)
1. NASCAR (Association)—History. 2. Stock car racing—United States—History.
3. Automobile racing drivers—United States—Biography. I. Title.
GV1029.9.S74G35 2008
796.720973—dc22

                                                              2007036609

Manufactured in the United States of America

On the cover: Jeff Gordon crosses the finish line on February 25, 2005, winning the NASCAR Nextel Cup Daytona 500. Gordon, driver of the #24 car, has been involved in some of the greatest moments in NASCAR history.

CONTENTS

Kevin Harvick, #29, leads NASCAR racers during the Nextel Cup Series Subway Fresh Fit 500 on April 21, 2007, in Avondale, Arizona.

INTRODUCTION

True NASCAR fans know that stock-car racing is about more than just driving fast. It's about champions who outrace the competition and still strive to top themselves. It's about underdogs who keep chasing the checkered flag and don't stop until they seize glory. It's about families devoted to victory, and about rivals who push each other to the limit. NASCAR is about speed, yes, but also about grit, determination, and triumph over tragedy. That's why NASCAR has given fans some of the most heart-stopping, breathtaking, spine-tingling moments in sports.

It all started in Daytona Beach, Florida. At the dawn of the twentieth century, racing enthusiasts gathered on the long, flat stretches of beach to shatter ground speed records. Daytona Beach would later become an important stock-car racetrack—and the home base of NASCAR.

Many early stock-car racers were involved in boot-legging during Prohibition, the period from 1920 to 1933

This crash occurred during a 1957 NASCAR race at Daytona Beach. Early NASCAR races were full of outlaws, weekend warriors, and backyard mechanics.

when the U.S. Constitution's 18th Amendment outlawed the sale, manufacture, and transportation of alcohol. Men who sold illegal alcohol, or bootleggers, had to outdrive the police to avoid arrest. Stock cars became a part of outlaw culture. When Prohibition ended, many former bootleggers began to race for fun.

Stock-car racing gradually gained popularity and became more mainstream, especially in America's southeastern states. In 1948, William France created the National Association for Stock Car Auto Racing: NASCAR. Today, the organization is a multibillion-dollar business, and NASCAR is one of America's most popular sports.

CHAPTER ONE

A Time of Legends

Until the 1970s, many racers were part-time enthusiasts who ran just a few races a year. But that didn't stop some of history's greatest drivers from burning rubber on NASCAR tracks.

The Silver Fox vs. the King

David Pearson was a genius behind the wheel. His ability to out-smart other drivers earned him the nickname "the Silver Fox." Pearson often didn't race a full season, but in the four years that he ran for the Winston Cup championship, he won three times! Pearson is famous for earning 105 career wins, the most in NASCAR history except for one man. That man was Pearson's greatest rival, Richard "King" Petty.

Petty was a record-setting machine: most career wins (200), most top-ten placings (712), and most pole positions (123) are just a few of his claims to fame. He won NASCAR's most important race, the Daytona 500, a record seven times. And, of course, Petty won seven career championships, a record equaled only by Dale Earnhardt.

GREAT MOMENTS IN NASCAR RACING

Pearson and Petty's rivalry was legendary. In 63 of the races in which they competed against each other, they took first and second place. Petty took first place 30 times, Pearson 33.

Outfoxed: The 1974 Firecracker 400

At the 1974 Firecracker 400, David Pearson famously "outfoxed" Richard Petty. As they entered the last lap of the race, Pearson was in the lead, with Petty running a close second. Pearson was worried that

"The Silver Fox," David Pearson, in his #21 car, crosses the finish line just ahead of Richard Petty (#43) at the 1974 Firecracker 400 in Daytona. Petty and Pearson were legendary rivals, finishing first and second in 63 races.

Pearson and Petty crashed into each other at the 1976 Daytona 500. Though both cars spun out, Pearson was able to inch slowly past the finish line, winning in surprising fashion.

Petty might try the famous "slingshot" move. To slingshot means to drive directly behind another car, letting it break wind resistance, and building up the momentum to pass. When the trailing car pulls out from behind the leader, it can speed ahead easily.

Pearson slowed down and pulled to the side, pretending to have blown out his engine. He even threw up his hands inside the car. Petty passed him, sure he had just won the race. But moments later, Pearson appeared large as life in Petty's rearview mirror. As they reached turn four of the last lap, Pearson slingshotted past Petty for the win.

Victory Crawl: *The 1976 Daytona 500*

The most celebrated race of the Pearson-Petty rivalry was the 1976 Daytona 500. On the last lap, Pearson took the lead, but his car climbed up the side of the track slightly. Petty drove below Pearson, trying to pull ahead on the inside. As Petty finally passed his rival, Pearson's car caught on Petty's ride and spun out. Trying to straighten himself out, Petty accidentally steered straight into the wall. He spun out of control, careening across the track and rolling onto the infield. His engine was dead.

Pearson spun onto the infield, too, but he popped his clutch at just the right moment. His engine was still running. He knew he could reach the finish line. Pearson and Petty had been driving so fast that they had left the other cars in the dust. Now, at about 20 miles per hour (32 kilometers per hour), Pearson crawled to victory. It was David Pearson's only win in the Daytona 500.

NASCAR Goes National: The 1979 Daytona 500

Until the late 1970s, NASCAR races were not nationally televised. Most stock-car racing fans were able to watch only highlights on ABC's popular television program *Wide World of Sports*. That all changed with the 1979 Daytona 500. It was the first NASCAR race to be televised live, flag to flag, on national television. The day of the race, a huge snowstorm hit the Northeast. Stuck at home in front of the television, thousands of Americans were about to get hooked on the drama and excitement of NASCAR.

It was a tough field of competitors. Legend Cale Yarborough, who had won the championship for the past three years running, was the man to beat. After 45 races without winning, Richard Petty was trying to claim another Daytona victory. And brothers Bobby and Donnie Allison were forces to be reckoned with.

As they entered the final lap, Yarborough and Donnie Allison went head to head. Leader Allison tried to force Yarborough into the muddy infield. As Yarborough struggled to get back onto the road, he pushed Allison up the side of the track—all the way into the wall. They both spun out into the infield, and Richard Petty drove on to win.

But Daytona's biggest story that day had nothing to do with victory. Bobby Allison drove to the infield, where his brother's car had stopped next to Yarborough's. Tempers flared. On national television, Yarborough and the Allison brothers got out of their cars screaming—and soon they were in an all-out fistfight. The TV cameras caught every second of the drama. The next day, the race and the fistfight were the talk of the nation. Everyone agreed that the fight was wrong, but it brought national attention to NASCAR for the first time. Petty's surprise win, the fight drama, and the huge new audience made the 1979 Daytona 500 the most important moment in NASCAR history.

Home of the Brave: The 1984 Firecracker 400

It was at the 1984 Firecracker 400 that NASCAR staked its claim as a truly national sport. The race was held on the Fourth of July, with a very special guest, President Ronald Reagan. He was the first sitting U.S. president to attend a NASCAR race.

It was an important race for Richard Petty: if he won, it would be his 200th victory. Toward the end of the race, Cale Yarborough and Petty were fighting for the lead. With two laps left to go, rookie Doug Heveron's car went into a semi-flip, and the yellow caution flag was raised. In those days, the yellow flag signaled all racers to return to the starting line, which they could do as fast as they wanted. As soon as they reached the start/finish line, however, the caution lap would begin, requiring each racer to slow down and hold his position. With just one lap left, the race wouldn't be restarted. It was all or nothing now: Petty and Yarborough knew that the first man back to the starting line would win.

GREAT MOMENTS IN NASCAR RACING

Yarborough slingshotted past Petty for the lead. But Petty kept driving hard, and in turn four he drew up right alongside Yarborough. The cars locked, sparks flew, and smoke billowed into the air. As the checkered flag waved, Petty won by mere inches.

According to the speech housed at the Ronald Regan Presidential Library, at the picnic following the race, President Reagan told the crowd: "I'm certain that if Jefferson and Adams and Washington were here with us today, they'd be sharing in the festivities. And if Patrick

After watching the Firecracker 400 on July 4, 1984, President Ronald Reagan congratulates racing legend Richard Petty on his 200th NASCAR win.

Henry were here, from what I've read about him, he'd have been out on the track with one of the cars."

Richard Petty had earned his 200th victory, but the historic win was also his last. Though he would race for eight more years, Petty would never win again.

The Rebel, the King, and the Kid: The 1992 Hooters 500

In 1992, the race for NASCAR's championship was so close that it all came down to one final race: the Hooters 500. Six men had a chance at winning the championship, including a rebel named Alan Kulwicki. Kulwicki was a NASCAR misfit: a mechanical engineer from Wisconsin who carried a briefcase to the garage. He owned his own racing team and refused to drive for wealthy owners who offered him better cars and more money. He even celebrated in a different way, by driving a "Polish victory lap" backward around the track. An underdog for the championship, Kulwicki got permission from Ford to change the name of his Ford Thunderbird to "Underbird."

The Hooters 500 began. An accident on lap 253 knocked out contender Davey Allison. Now only Bill Elliott and Kulwicki had a shot at the championship. These two great drivers were very close in points; the championship would be won by a razor-thin margin. Kulwicki realized that whoever led the most laps in this race would receive five bonus points, enough to give him the championship. Although Elliott won the actual race, and Kulwicki took second, Kulwicki had led 103 laps, one more than Elliott's 102. Just a single lap made Kulwicki NASCAR's new champion. He became the first northerner, the first

Owner-driver Alan Kulwicki works on his #7 car before a March 1993 race in South Carolina.

college graduate, and the last owner-driver to win the championship. At his awards banquet later that year, NASCAR honored him by playing Frank Sinatra's "My Way."

Tragically, Kulwicki died in a plane crash just months later. Every winner for the whole 1993 season honored Kulwicki with a Polish victory lap.

The 1992 Hooters 500 race was also significant for other reasons. It was the last race for racing legend Richard Petty and the first for a young unknown driver named Jeff Gordon. NASCAR was about to enter a whole new era of intense competition.

CHAPTER TWO

The Intimidator

Richard Petty might lay claim to most of NASCAR's major records. But without a doubt, stock-car racing's most famous icon is Dale Earnhardt Sr. Born in Kannapolis, North Carolina, Dale was the son of early NASCAR great Ralph Earnhardt. Dale made his NASCAR Winston Cup debut in 1975, at the age of 24. He was a strong competitor from the beginning, earning NASCAR's Rookie of the Year Award in 1979. He took home his first championship the very next season. To this day, he's still the only driver to have won a championship in his sophomore season. He earned the nickname "the Intimidator" for his all-or-nothing driving style, and "the Man in Black" for the black paint scheme his famous #3 car often sported.

The "Pass in the Grass": the 1987 Winston All-Star Challenge

One of Earnhardt's greatest rivals was the legendary Bill Elliott. Elliott became know as "Million Dollar Bill" in 1985, when he won three of NASCAR's four biggest races—at Daytona, Talladega, and Darlington—to receive the very first Winston Million bonus.

Dale Earnhardt Sr. waves to his fans after a win at the Busch Classic in 1986. Earnhardt's all-out driving style and total commitment to winning by any means necessary earned him the nickname "the Intimidator."

In 1987, Earnhardt's rivalry with Elliott came to a head at the Winston All-Star race. Elliott led the pack for 121 of 125 laps. Earnhardt bided his time until the end of the race. When a crash opened up the field a bit, he steered around other cars to seize the lead. Elliott, furious, drove very close to Earnhardt's bumper. The two cars made contact and Earnhardt was pushed out into the grass. Earnhardt didn't give up, however. He made tracks through 150 feet (46 meters) of grass and mud, all the way back to the road, and kept barreling toward the finish line. Elliott, furious once again, pulled up alongside Earnhardt in turn three. Earnhardt nudged him against the wall. Elliott's fender bent, his tire was damaged, and he lost his lead.

Not all drivers—and not all fans—liked the Intimidator's attitude. He was often booed at tracks. That year, NASCAR president Bill France Jr. warned Earnhardt to get serious about his safety and the safety of other drivers. Earnhardt agreed and was as good as his word. Later in 1987, Earnhardt earned his third NASCAR championship.

True Grit: The 1996 DieHard 500

Earnhardt wasn't always victorious. He went through "drought" periods without wins, survived horrible crashes, and faced personal tragedies. But he never gave up and never stopped trying. His resolve was sometimes astonishing.

One of Dale Earnhardt's biggest challenges came during the 1996 DieHard 500 at Talladega Superspeedway in Talladega, Alabama. A spectacular crash turned Earnhardt's car on its side. It skated and spun along the track on one of its doors. The car then turned upside down, got hit by other cars, and finally turned right side up again before stopping. It was a miracle that Earnhardt walked away with only a broken sternum and collarbone. His injuries, however, did threaten to bench him for the rest of the season. In his next race, the Brickyard 400, Earnhardt's injuries forced him to leave his car just as the race had begun.

Amazingly, in the qualifying laps for the very next race, the Bud at the Glen at Watkins Glen International, Earnhardt took the pole and set a track record. Soon Earnhardt fans were wearing T-shirts proclaiming "It Hurt So Good." Earnhardt came in sixth at Watkins Glen, but his grit and determination made him first in the hearts of fans.

Above, Dale Earnhardt Sr.'s and Sterling Marlin's cars crash during the 1996 DieHard 500 at Talladega. The cars were racing at speeds nearing 200 miles per hour (322 kilometers per hour), and the cars were totaled. Earnhardt was lucky that he wasn't more seriously injured.

Daytona Dreams

By 1998, Dale Earnhardt had tied Richard Petty's record of seven championships. He had claimed victories at all of NASCAR's greatest tracks. Only one prize still eluded him: NASCAR's most important race, the Daytona 500.

Dale Earnhardt's bad luck at the Daytona 500 was legendary. In 1986, just three laps from the checkered flag, he ran out of gas. In 1990, he cut a tire on turn three of the last lap. In 1995, Earnhardt went from fourteenth place to second in the final ten laps of the race but couldn't beat Sterling Marlin for the win.

By the time the 1998 Daytona 500 rolled around, Dale Earnhardt had been trying—and failing—to win the Great American Race for 20 years. To make matters worse, he was also going through a drought: it had been 59 races since he had earned a trip to victory lane.

The "Icing on the Cake": The 1998 Daytona 500

Just before the 1998 Daytona 500, a young girl in a wheelchair gave Dale Earnhardt a lucky penny. Earnhardt taped it to his dashboard. And this time, nothing went wrong. After 140 laps, Earnhardt held on to the lead. As if in a dream, he easily fended off Bobby Labonte, and suddenly, he had won. The crowd went wild.

It was a victory 20 years in the making, and the post-race celebration was the stuff of NASCAR legend. As Earnhardt drove onto pit road, every member of every crew came out to congratulate "the Man in Black" in an unprecedented show of respect. As the receiving line ended, Earnhardt spun himself out onto the infield. His doughnuts in the grass wrote a giant number three—the number of his famous car. When Earnhardt finally got to victory lane, an article by Bob Zeller in the North Carolina *News & Record* quotes him as telling reporters, "It's just unbelievable that you could win another race and feel more excited than you feel about the last one, but the Daytona 500 tops them all . . . It tops all the last 30 races I've won here . . . It puts the icing on the cake."

Even after winning the prize he coveted most, Dale Earnhardt stayed hungry and remained dominant. The world of NASCAR still remembers the 2000 Winston 500 at Talladega, when Dale Earnhardt smoked past the competition, going from 18th place

After his historic 1998 Daytona 500 victory, Dale Earnhardt Sr. makes his mark on the infield. Earnhardt drove a few doughnuts in the grass, leaving behind tiremarks in the shape of a huge #3, the number of his legendary car.

all the way to first in under five laps—winning the Winston Million bonus.

NASCAR's Worst Moment: The 2001 Daytona 500

On February 18, 2001, Dale Earnhardt entered the Daytona 500 again. Little did he know that this time would be his last.

As the Daytona 500 drew to a close, Dale Earnhardt Sr. was in third place. Ahead of him were his son, Dale Earnhardt Jr., and Michael Waltrip, two drivers for his own team, Dale Earnhardt Incorporated.

In turn four of the last lap, Sterling Marlin bumped Earnhardt Sr. slightly. Struggling to correct himself, Earnhardt steered up the side of the track. He crossed the path of Ken Schrader, who hit him. Schrader and Earnhardt hit the concrete wall noses first. It didn't look like a terrible wreck—Earnhardt had been through worse. But a few hours later, NASCAR president Mike Helton told the world sadly: "We've lost Dale Earnhardt."

Across the United States, Earnhardt's tragic death made front-page news. The fans' outpouring of grief was incredible. Though the

This fan-made memorial at the Atlanta Motor Speedway in Hampton, Georgia, was just one of the many expressions of grief that followed Dale Earnhardt Sr.'s death in February 2001. His death was a turning point for NASCAR, leading the organization to improve driver safety.

Intimidator had been both loved and hated during his lifetime, now that he was gone, America realized how much the Man in Black had meant to millions.

The tragedy transformed NASCAR. Two huge investigations found that a variety of factors had combined to seal Earnhardt's fate, including a torn seatbelt and the speed and angle of his collision with the wall. NASCAR responded with a new focus on safety. Head and neck restraints that could have saved Earnhardt's life were introduced. Other safety improvements followed. Earnhardt's death also inspired the creation of "the Car of Tomorrow," a new standard NASCAR model designed to be safer, less expensive, and more competitive. The Car of Tomorrow debuted on NASCAR tracks in 2007.

A NASCAR Miracle: The Cracker Barrel Old Country Store 500

Earnhardt was replaced at Richard Childress Racing (although Earnhardt set up his own team, Dale Earnhardt Incorporated, in 1980, he raced for Childress until his death) by rookie Kevin Harvick. Just three weeks after Earnhardt's death, the Intimidator's grieving fans saw Harvick win the Cracker Barrel Old Country Store 500. He was driving a car that had been built for Earnhardt. It was only Harvick's third Nextel Cup race, but he managed to beat Earnhardt's great rival Jeff Gordon by 0.006 of a second. The rookie drove to victory lane holding up three fingers—the number of Earnhardt's immortal car. The crowd went wild.

Even greater moments for Earnhardt fans would come with Dale Earnhardt Jr.'s triumphs at Daytona, at the site of his father's biggest victories and worst tragedy.

CHAPTER THREE

Fathers and Sons

Stock-car racing often runs in the family. A successful racer needs to know stock cars inside and out. Growing up spending time in a garage helps. A racing family is also likely to provide early experience, such as putting an eager child behind the wheel of a go-kart or a dirt bike. And a great racer needs inspiration, like a racing father, brother, or sister to look up to.

From the Pettys, Earnhardts, Waltrips, and Allisons to the Labontes, Busches, and Burtons, stock-car-racing families have made speed their family tradition.

The Alabama Gang: The Allisons

Brothers Bobby and Donnie Allison started racing during the 1960s. Like many earlier NASCAR drivers, they lived race to race, using their winnings to pay their next race entry fee. Their quest to find a racing home base led them to Hueytown, Alabama, near Talladega Superspeedway. The brothers set up shop there with their friend Red Farmer and were soon known as the Alabama Gang. Donnie became a

Bobby Allison (right) and his son Davey (left) loved to race each other. This photo was taken after a 1998 practice for the Miller High Life 500 at Pocono International Raceway.

great racer, but it was Bobby who claimed true legend status. Bobby won the NASCAR championship in 1983 and won the Daytona 500 three times.

The Allisons' Next Generation

Bobby's sons, Davey and Clifford, both followed in his footsteps. Bobby was a loving father, but he was never easy on his boys. He didn't give them fancy equipment. If they wanted to be stock-car drivers, they would have to build their own cars, like he did.

Davey, in particular, showed promise as one of NASCAR's most talented young drivers. He started working in the garage at age 12. His father warned him that he couldn't start racing until he graduated high school, so Davey attended summer school in order to graduate early. Davey won NASCAR Rookie of the Year in 1987, scoring two wins in his first full season.

Father Knows Best: The 1988 Daytona 500

The Allison family's greatest moment came during the 1998 Daytona 500. With 14 laps left to go, engine trouble forced Darrell Waltrip out of the running. Waltrip and Bobby Allison had been battling for most of the race. Now, the race became father against son—Bobby vs. Davey.

On the final lap, Davey looked like he might overtake his father. However, Bobby pulled away and won by two car lengths. At age 50,

Bobby Allison became the oldest driver to win the Daytona 500. But more important, he and his son finished first and second. According to an article by Mark Aumann, on NASCAR.com, Davey told reporters, "Since I was a kid, I've dreamed about battling to the wire, finishing 1–2 with my dad. The only difference was, I wanted him to finish second."

A Father's Pride: The Jarretts

Racing legend Ned Jarrett didn't come from a racing family. His father thought of stock-car racers as bootleggers and hillbillies. Only when Ned started winning races under a fake name did his father finally give him permission to compete.

The first few years of racing were hard for Ned. He paid for one of his race cars—purchased from legend Junior Johnson—with a check for $2,000, written just after the bank closed so it would not bounce. That weekend, Ned used his new car to win two races and raise the money to pay for it. He went on to become a two-time Grand National champion. In retirement, he launched a second career as an important racing announcer on television and radio.

Dale and Glenn Jarrett, Ned's two sons, grew up very differently. Their friends were the children of drivers David Pearson, Bobby Allison, and Richard Petty. Ned Jarrett, who knew his profession was dangerous, discouraged his sons from racing. Still, the Jarrett boys both tried their luck behind the wheel. Glenn eventually became a racing announcer. Dale raced.

Dale Jarrett spent four long years in the Winston Cup Series before he earned his first victory. It was his 129th career start. When the win finally came, it was followed by another long drought. Dale didn't win again that year, or the next. By the time that the 1993 season began, it was clear that Dale Jarrett had talent—but did he have the right stuff to become a true champion?

Dale vs. Dale: The 1993 Daytona 500

Many NASCAR fans predicted that the 1993 Daytona 500 would belong to another Dale: Dale Earnhardt Sr. But Dale Jarrett intended to give the Intimidator a run for his money.

Jarrett didn't come close to victory until the very end of the Daytona 500. With two laps left to go, Earnhardt was still winning. But Dale Jarrett saw an opening beneath rookie Jeff Gordon and swooped into it, pulling up alongside Earnhardt. The two cars bumped together. Both were close to victory, but Earnhardt's car slid slightly up the track, allowing Jarrett to pull ahead.

Dale Jarrett's dad, Ned, was covering the race from the CBS broadcast booth. As the race zoomed toward its conclusion, the director told Ned Jarrett to call the race his son was so close to winning. According to an article by Tom Gillispie in the *Winston-Salem Journal*, Ned Jarrett cheered on national radio: "It's the Dale and Dale Show, and you know who I'm pulling for, Dale Jarrett!" As millions of Americans listened, Ned Jarrett rooted for his son, yelled out advice, and celebrated as, against all odds, Dale Jarrett took the checkered flag. Dale Jarrett had won the Great American Race by just 0.16 seconds.

Ned Jarrett was usually very professional on the air, and he was embarrassed by his behavior. He later apologized to the Intimidator for rooting for his son on the radio. In the *Winston-Salem Journal* article, Ned Jarrett remembered, "[Earnhardt] pointed a finger at me, and he said, 'Don't you forget that I'm a daddy, too.'"

In 1999, Dale Jarrett became a NASCAR champion himself, making the Jarretts NASCAR's second pair of father-son Winston Cup champions (after Lee and Richard Petty).

Dale Jarrett (#18) speeds to victory in the 1993 Daytona 500, despite tough competition from Dale Earnhardt Sr., the Man in Black (#3). Jarrett's father, sports commentator Ned Jarrett, announced the race on national radio.

Living Up to a Legend: The Earnhardts

When Dale Earnhardt Sr. died in 2001, he left behind incredible records and great racing memories. But he also left NASCAR with a living legacy: his son, Dale Earnhardt Jr.

"Junior" started his professional racing career in 1999, at age 17. He won back-to-back Busch Series championships before his rookie year on the 2000 Winston Cup circuit. He scored two victories and won two poles in his first 16 rookie races, matching Davey Allison's modern-era record. His daddy was proud.

Unfortunately, Dale Senior didn't get to race his son for long. The next year, Dale Earnhardt Sr. died in a crash at the Daytona 500 (Michael Waltrip, brother of NASCAR great Darrell Waltrip, and

Dale Junior finished first and second in the race). Many of Dale Senior's fans transferred their hopes and prayers to his son, who continued racing despite his grief.

"He Was with Me Tonight": The 2001 Pepsi 400

The NASCAR world was traumatized by the loss of the Man in Black. The Intimidator had been a major racer for so long that competing without him felt wrong. Emotions ran high as NASCAR prepared to return to Daytona, the scene of his tragic death, for the first time during the 2001 Pepsi 400.

It was a tough race, but it was clear to everyone that Dale Earnhardt Jr. intended to dominate. On the final restart of the race, after a pit stop, Earnhardt Jr. was in sixth place. There were six laps left to go. NASCAR fans watched, amazed, as Junior passed every car in front of him. It was great driving—just like his dad.

There was more déjà vu in store. In the final two laps, a new car caught up to Dale Junior—his teammate, Michael Waltrip. In Dale Earnhardt Sr.'s last race, he had helped Waltrip win his first Daytona 500. Now Waltrip was going to help Dale Junior make his daddy proud. Waltrip fended off the field of cars, making sure that Junior kept his lead. The crowd leapt to its feet as Junior drove to victory.

It was a storybook ending to a NASCAR nightmare. Earnhardt Jr. and Waltrip drove into the infield and climbed on top of their cars, celebrating with friends and crew. In victory lane, Junior told reporters, "He was with me tonight. I don't know how he did it, but he did it."

Junior's Triumph: The 2004 Daytona 500

But Earnhardt Jr.'s biggest win yet was still ahead. Exactly six years after his father finally won his only Daytona 500, Junior won the Great American Race. It was only his fifth try.

Dale Earnhardt Jr., in the #8 car, finishes first in the 2001 Pepsi 400 at Daytona. It was the first race at the track since his father's tragic death. It is still remembered as one of the most emotional wins in NASCAR history.

Junior had already experienced a fraction of his father's Daytona frustrations. In 2002, a damaged tire kept Dale Junior from winning the Daytona 500. In 2003, his alternator was the problem. But in 2004, it seemed that nothing could hold him back. He and his crew had worked long and hard through the off-season to build the best car they could. With 19 laps left to go in the race, Dale Earnhardt Jr. pulled ahead of Tony Stewart. He held on to first place and won by a large margin.

Earnhardt Junior was mobbed by his family, friends, and crew. It was a momentous celebration. He flashed three fingers to the adoring crowd. No one could deny that he had earned his victory. In victory lane, Tony Stewart told reporters, "Considering what this kid went through losing his father here at the Daytona 500, and knowing how good he's been here . . . it's nice to see him get his victory here, too.

Tony Stewart congratulates Dale Earnhardt Jr. on seizing victory in the 2004 Daytona 500. The race held special meaning for Earnhardt: Daytona International Speedway was the scene of his legendary father's greatest frustrations and victories, as well as his tragic death.

I think his father's really proud today . . . If I could have held [Junior] off, had him finish second, I would have done it in a heartbeat. But there was no holding that kid back today. Today was his day." As for Dale Junior, he told the press, "He was over in the passenger side with me. I'm sure he was having a blast."

CHAPTER FOUR

A New Generation

In NASCAR's early days, big stars dominated easily. These days, top competitors are driving amazing cars, and it's never been tougher to seize victory. Welcome to today's NASCAR: unpredictable and nothing less than thrilling.

Take this example from Darlington Speedway, during the 1993 Carolina Dodge Dealers 400. In the last two laps, it was a duel between Kurt Busch and Ricky Craven. They weaved around each other, slammed each other into the wall, and battled all the way around the track. As the finish line loomed near, Busch and Craven locked together and passed the finish line door to door. Craven won by mere inches— just 0.002 seconds, the closest margin in NASCAR history.

"Wonder Boy": Jeff Gordon

Jeff Gordon is a new breed of NASCAR driver. He was born in Vallejo, California, far from the southeastern home of NASCAR. His family moved to Pittsboro, Indiana, so Jeff could start racing at a young age. Gordon was 22 when he became a Winston Cup rookie, but he'd already been racing for years. Maybe that's why he started winning big so early in his career. Just two days after his 23rd birthday, in August 1994, Gordon won the very first NASCAR race ever held at his adopted home track, the legendary Indianapolis Motor Speedway. The speedway is famous for being the home of America's most important open-wheel race, the Indianapolis 500.

Nicknamed "Wonder Boy" by Dale Earnhardt Sr., Gordon won the NASCAR championship in 1995 and 1996. In 1998, he won 13 races, seven poles, and 28 top-ten finishes, plus the championship—one of the most incredible seasons in NASCAR history.

A Rock and a Hard Place: The 1999 Daytona 500

Gordon proved his daring and determination at the 1999 Daytona 500. With 11 laps left in the race, Rusty Wallace was the leader. Going into turn two, Gordon decided to dive below Wallace and snatch the lead. But at the last minute, Gordon saw that there was already another car below Wallace. Ricky Rudd was inching along the bottom of the track in his damaged car, racking up points for laps finished. There wasn't a lot of room in between Wallace and Rudd. Wallace drove closer to Rudd, warning Gordon to stay away. What would Gordon do?

As Gordon dove into the narrow space between the two cars, the crowd held its breath, expecting to see a big crash. Gordon just barely squeezed through, and he shot into the lead. But he wasn't home free yet—he still had to face the Intimidator. Dale Earnhardt Sr. drove up behind him, swerving left and right, looking for a way to get past. But Wonder Boy refused to surrender and never gave up his lead.

Jeff Gordon is still a major NASCAR contender. In 2001, he won a fourth championship. Then, in 2007, Gordon shattered two major

Jeff Gordon's iconic rainbow-colored #24 car races to a first-place finish in the 1999 Daytona 500.

records: Darrell Waltrip's modern-day record of 59 poles and Dale Earnhardt Sr.'s modern-day record of 76 career wins.

The Driver's Driver: Tony Stewart

Indiana native Tony Stewart is considered by many fans to be the purest driving talent in NASCAR today. Before entering NASCAR's top level, he raced any vehicle he could get his hands on. He won championships in go-karts, sprint cars, midget cars, and open-wheel race cars.

Before becoming a full-time NASCAR driver, Stewart also raced at the highest level of American open-wheel racing in the Indy Racing League. In fact, he won the IndyCar championship in 1997 while also racing in NASCAR's Busch Series.

All of Stewart's experience paid off when he finally reached NASCAR's Winston Cup Series. He won Rookie of the Year in 1999 and won his first Winston Cup championship in 2002.

Home Sweet Home: The 2005 Brickyard 400

Tony Stewart grew up dreaming of winning a big race at his home track, Indianapolis Motor Speedway (nicknamed "the Brickyard," home of the Indianapolis 500). First in the Indy Racing League (IRL), and later in NASCAR, his dream eluded him. Winning at Indianapolis became an obsession for Stewart. After leaving the IRL and becoming a full-time NASCAR driver, he still competed in the Indianapolis 500, even though that meant racing in Indiana in the morning, then flying to Charlotte, North Carolina, to race in the Coca-Cola 600 later that night! An IRL and NASCAR champion, Stewart had never won the race that meant the most to him. Until the 2005 Brickyard 400, that is.

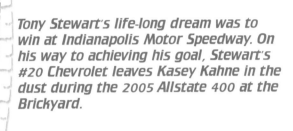

Tony Stewart's life-long dream was to win at Indianapolis Motor Speedway. On his way to achieving his goal, Stewart's #20 Chevrolet leaves Kasey Kahne in the dust during the 2005 Allstate 400 at the Brickyard.

On lap 100, with 60 laps to go, Tony Stewart took over the lead. For a moment, it looked like Kasey Kahne might steal his thunder and disappoint all of Stewart's hometown fans. But Stewart grabbed the lead again on lap 150 and won by five car lengths. Stewart knelt to kiss the bricks at the track he had worked so hard to tame. The icing on the cake came later that year, when Stewart won his second championship.

Young Wolf: Jimmie Johnson

One of the hottest young NASCAR stars is El Cajon, California, native Jimmie Johnson. An avid racer who spent most of his early life behind the wheel, Johnson became the first rookie ever to lead the point standings. In his first five seasons, he finished in the top five in points, the only driver to claim that distinction.

In 2004, Johnson missed winning the Nextel Cup championship by just eight points—the closest margin in NASCAR history—even though he won four of the season's last six races. By 2006, although he had been racing in the NASCAR's premier series for only four years, people had grown accustomed to his talent. He was always winning races and poles, always collecting lots of points. So why hadn't he won a championship yet?

Never Say Never: *The 2006 Ford 400*

In 2006, Johnson won his first Daytona 500. He went on to win other important 2006 races: the Aaron's 499 at Talladega, the All-Star Challenge, and the Allstate 400 at the Brickyard.

But the 2006 championship was far from a sure thing for Johnson. At the beginning of "the Chase," NASCAR's "playoffs," he crashed at New Hampshire International Speedway. In a couple of races, Johnson even finished outside the top ten. He fell to ninth place in the standings. Others might have given up, but Johnson was undeterred. He put his nose to the grindstone and worked his way back to the Chase's top slot.

Then came the Ford 400 at the Homestead-Miami Speedway. Johnson needed a 12th-place finish or better to clinch the title. At the very beginning of the race, a spring fell off Kurt Busch's car and cut a huge hole in the nose of Johnson's Chevrolet. Johnson's crew patched up the hole with tape, but emergency pit stops take time. When Johnson reentered the race, he was in 40th place.

The next 60 laps were a lesson in sheer determination as Jimmie Johnson passed 29 other cars. He kept his cool, dodging to steer clear of spinning drivers, always keeping his eye on the prize. He even stayed focused during a pit mishap when the final lug nut on one of his tires wasn't fully attached.

Johnson didn't win the race. He didn't place 12th, either. He placed ninth, securing his place as NASCAR's 2006 Nextel Cup champion.

Jimmie Johnson (#48) seizes his first NASCAR championship at the 2006 Ford 400 in Homestead, Florida. Johnson showed great determination over the course of the race, driving from 40th place at one point to a ninth-place finish.

Great Moments of the Future

Hopefully, great drivers like Jeff Gordon, Tony Stewart, Jimmie Johnson, Matt Kenseth, Kurt Busch, and Dale Earnhardt Jr. will keep wowing crowds across the United States. Will Jeff Gordon equal or break Earnhardt's record and win seven championships—or even eight? Will Dale Earnhardt Jr. follow in his father's footsteps as a remarkable NASCAR champion? There's a lot to look forward to in years to come. Meanwhile, fans are wondering how NASCAR will change. The Car of Tomorrow, intended to level the playing field for drivers and make racing safer, was introduced in 2007. How will it transform the sport?

GREAT MOMENTS IN NASCAR RACING

There has also been a lot of talk in NASCAR about greater diversity among its drivers. NASCAR pioneer Wendell Scott is still the only African American driver to win a NASCAR event on the highest level. Aviation engineer Janet Guthrie made history in 1976, when she became the first woman to compete in a Winston Cup event. However, a major female star is still on the horizon for NASCAR. Who will be the first to break down these barriers? And who will be the next wonder rookie to take the racing world by storm?

Jeff Gordon drives his #24 Chevrolet during practice laps for the 3M Performance 400 at Michigan International Speedway in August 2007. Future NASCAR seasons will bring untold thrills and surprises.

Who will be the underdog who shocks the world by proving his or her excellence? What will be the next moment of sheer sporting excitement that keeps fans talking for decades?

These questions will all be answered in time. This much is certain, however: many great moments are yet to come. And stock-car racing will keep delivering thrills, year after year, generation after generation.

GLOSSARY

bootlegger During Prohibition in the United States (1920–1933), a person engaged in making, transporting, or selling illegal alcohol.

Busch Series NASCAR's "minor leagues." Many Nextel Cup racers hone their skills in the Busch Series before moving on to NASCAR's highest level of competition.

caution In car racing, when an accident, debris on the track, or bad weather makes racing hazardous, referees call a caution period by waving a yellow flag. Currently, when the caution flag is displayed, all racers must slow down to the speed of the pace car and stay in their current positions.

the Chase A type of "playoffs" for NASCAR, introduced during the 2004 season. As of 2007, after the first 26 races of the season, the top 12 teams have their points reset for the season's last ten races. The team with the highest points at the end of the season wins.

checkered flag The flag signaling that the race is over. To "take the checkered flag" means to win a race.

Daytona 500 This race, also called the Great American Race, is the first and most important race of the NASCAR season. The race is held at Daytona International Speedway in Daytona Beach, Florida.

go-karts Small open-wheel carts that race on small courses. Many young racers begin their careers in go-karts.

Indianapolis Motor Speedway The home of American open-wheel racing and one of the most important race tracks in America. It is nicknamed "the Brickyard" because in the track's early years it was paved with bricks.

Indy Racing League The sanctioning body for the prestigious IndyCar open-wheel racing series. The Indianapolis 500 is the most important race on the Indy Racing League schedule.

midget cars Race cars with powerful engines but very small bodies.

modern era NASCAR's modern era began in 1972, when changes to NASCAR's rules, finances, and promotional strategy made the sport richer and more competitive.

Nextel Cup/Winston Cup NASCAR's highest level of competition. It has been renamed several times since 1949: In 1970, it was named the Winston Cup to honor sponsor R. J. Reynolds Tobacco. In 2004, new sponsor Nextel Communications gave its name to the Nextel Cup.

open-wheel An open-wheel race car has wheels outside of its main body. Open-wheel cars are built expressly for racing and are not meant to resemble "street" cars. Until recently, some considered open-wheel racing to be more prestigious than stock-car racing.

pole position The best starting spot in a race. In NASCAR, the car with the fastest qualifying time earns the pole position.

sprint cars Small but powerful open-wheel cars designed to race on short tracks. Many NASCAR drivers gain experience in sprint cars before racing stock cars.

stock car Technically, a stock car is a mass-manufactured vehicle available to the public. But in the racing world, "stock cars" are sophisticated race cars loosely based on automobiles available to the public.

Winston Million bonus A $1 million cash prize awarded by NASCAR sponsor R. J. Reynolds Tobacco to drivers who won three of four events: the Daytona 500, the Winston 500, the Coca-Cola 600, and the Southern 500. The prize proved so hard to win that it was offered only from 1985 to 1997 and was later replaced by other awards.

Daytona International Speedway
1801 W. International Speedway Boulevard
Daytona Beach, FL 32114
(386) 254-2700
Web site: http://www.daytonainternationalspeedway.com
Daytona International Speedway is the home of NASCAR's most
important race, the Daytona 500.

Motorsports Hall of Fame of America
P.O. Box 194
Novi, MI 48376-0194
(800) 250-RACE (7223)
Web site: http://www.mshf.com
The Motorsports Hall of Fame hosts exhibits on some of the best
drivers in stock-car and open-wheel racing, as well as motorcycling,
drag racing, sports cars, air racing, and power boats.

National Association for Stock Car Auto Racing, Inc. (NASCAR)
P.O. Box 2875
Daytona Beach, FL 32120
Web site: http://www.nascar.com
NASCAR is the official sanctioning body for stock-car racing in the
United States. It consists of three major national series (the Nextel
Cup, Busch, and Craftsman Truck series) as well as eight
regional series.

Victory Junction Gang Camp
4500 Adam's Way

Randleman, NC 27317

(877) VJG-CAMP (854-2267) or (366) 498-9055

Web site: http://www.victoryjunction.org

Victory Junction Gang Camp is a NASCAR-themed camp for children with serious or life-threatening illnesses. It was founded in honor of deceased racer Adam Petty, Richard Petty's grandson, and is supported by many NASCAR fans.

WEB SITES

Due to the changing nature of Internet links, Rosen Publishing has developed an online list of Web sites related to the subject of this book. This site is updated regularly. Please use this link to access the list:

http://www.rosenlinks.com/hnr/gmnr

FOR FURTHER READING

Buckley, James. *NASCAR* (Eyewitness Books). New York, NY: DK Children's Books, 2005.

Garner, Joe. *Speed, Guts, & Glory: 100 Unforgettable Moments in NASCAR History*. New York, NY: Grand Central Publishing, 2006.

Moriarty, Frank. *Dynasties: Legendary Families of Stock Car Racing*. New York, NY: Metrobooks, 2002.

NASCAR Scene editors. *Thunder and Glory: The 25 Most Memorable Races in NASCAR Winston Cup History* (NASCAR Library Collection). Chicago, IL: Triumph Books, 2004.

Poole, David, and Jim McLaurin. *NASCAR Essential: Everything You Need to Know to Be a Real Fan!* Chicago, IL: Triumph Books, 2007.

Poole, David, and Jim McLaurin. *"Then Junior Said to Jeff . . .": The Best NASCAR Stories Ever Told*. Chicago, IL: Triumph Books, 2006.

BIBLIOGRAPHY

The Associated Press. "NASCAR Recalls Petty Milestone; 200th Career Win Came 20 Years Ago." *Grand Rapids Press*, July 4, 2004, p. B9.

Aumann, Mark. "1979: Petty Winds Up in 'Fist' Place." NASCAR.com. January 23, 2003. Retrieved May 26, 2007 (http://www.nascar.com/2003/kyn/history/daytona/01/23/daytona_1979).

Aumann, Mark. "1988: Father Before Son." NASCAR.com. February 1, 2003. Retrieved May 26, 2007 (http://www.nascar.com/2003/kyn/history/daytona/01/31/daytona_1988/index.html).

Brinster, Dick. "Jarrett Breaks Through: Father Is Proud of Dale's Success." *Daily News*, June 16, 1996, p. SB1.

CNN/Sports Illustrated.com. "'The Pass': Even Gordon Impressed by Daring Maneuver." February 26, 1997. Retrieved May 29, 2007 (http://robots.cnnsi.com/motorsports/1999/daytona500/news/1999/02/15/daytona_follow/).

Duarte, Joseph. "It's the Big D for Little E: Earnhardt Jr. Wins First Daytona 500 on Fifth Try." *Houston Chronicle*, February 16, 2004, p 1.

El-Bashir, Tarik. "Indy Win Marks Stewart's 'Best Day.'" *Washington Post*, August 8, 2005.

Gillispie, Tom. "Families: Blood Is Thicker than Oil in Racing." *Winston-Salem Journal*, October 11, 2003, p. F4.

Harris, Mike. "New Champion Enters—and Old One Departs." *Albany Times Union*, November 16, 1992, p. D1.

Jenkins, Chris. "Junior's Win Kicks Off New NASCAR Era." *USA Today*, February 15, 2004. Retrieved May 2007 (http://www.usatoday.com/sports/motor/nascar/2004-02-15-daytona_x.htm).

Korth, Joanne. "The Year That Changed NASCAR." *St. Petersburg Times*, February 8, 2002, p. 1C.

Long, Dustin. "Storybook Ending Has Son Shining Again." *Virginian Pilot*, July 9, 2001, p. C1.

McLaughlin, Matt. "Racing at the Beach: Earnhardt Tries His Best . . . and Comes Up Short, 1990–93." Frontstretch.com. February 12, 2007. Retrieved May 26, 2007 (http://www.frontstretch.com/mmclaughlin/6921).

Minter, Rick. "How Dale Earnhardt Died: Several Factors Came Together at Precisely the Wrong Moment." *Atlanta Journal-Constitution*, August 22, 2001, p. A1.

Minter, Rick. "Tragedy for a Racing Family: Sons, Team Are Earnhardt's Legacy. Dale Earnhardt 1951–2001." *Atlanta Journal-Constitution*, February 19, 2001, p. C8.

NASCAR.com. "The 1976 Daytona 500." July 28, 2003. Retrieved May 26, 2007 (http://www.nascar.com/2002/kyn/history/races/02/02/76daytona500/index.html).

NASCAR.com. "2003 Carolina Dodge Dealers 400: What a Duel." July 28, 2003. Retrieved May 28, 2007 (http://www.nascar.com/2003/kyn/history/races/04/02/craven_busch_2003/index.html).

Phillips, Benny. "Bobby Allison—NASCAR Racing—Pit Stop for a Look Back." *Stock Car Racing*, January 2006. Retrieved May 2007 (http://www.stockcarracing.com/featurestories/scrp_0601_bobby_allison).

Ronald Reagan Presidential Library. "Remarks at a Picnic Following the Pepsi Firecracker 400 in Daytona Beach, Florida, July 4, 1984." Retrieved May 25, 2007 (http://www.reagan.utexas.edu/archives/speeches/1984/70484c.htm).

Ryan, Nate. "Johnson Wraps Up Nextel Cup Championship." *USA Today*, November 19, 2006. Retrieved May 2007 (http://www.usatoday.com/sports/motor/nascar/2006-11-19-homestead_x.htm).

Salisbury, Jim. "Earnhardt Is Gone, but Hardly Forgotten." *Philadelphia Inquirer*, February 19, 2006.

Smith, Marty. "2001 Cracker Barrel 500: An Angel Among Us." NASCAR.com. July 28, 2003. Retrieved May 28, 2007 (http://www.nascar.com/2002/kyn/history/races/12/12/2001_atlanta/index.html).

Tays, Alan. "He Was with Me Tonight." *Palm Beach Post*, July 8, 2001, p. 1C.

TonyStewart.com. "Tony Stewart Biography." Retrieved May 29, 2007 (www.tonystewart.com/bio).

Waid, Steve. "1998 Daytona 500: At Last Earnhardt Wins Daytona 500." The Earnhardt Connection. 2001. Retrieved May 26, 2007 (http://www.daleearnhardt.net/history/98daytona/index.htm).

Zeller, Bob. "Biggest Victory; Feb. 15 1998; Daytona 500; Daytona International Speedway." *News & Record*, February 23, 2001, p. 9.

INDEX

About the Author

Sally Ganchy is a writer, teaching artist, and curriculum designer. Originally from Fort Smith, Arkansas, she is a dedicated NASCAR fan. In her spare time, Ganchy is a bluegrass fiddler who enjoys jazz, world music, and opera. She currently lives in Budapest, Hungary, where keeping up with NASCAR is an important way of staying in touch with home.

Photo Credits

Designer: Nelson Sá
Photo Researcher: Marty Levick